Sustainable Wellbeing

Tracy De Geer

BALBOA.
PRESS

A DIVISION OF HAY HOUSE

Balboa Press books may be ordered through booksellers or by contacting:

Balboa Press
A Division of Hay House
1663 Liberty Drive
Bloomington, IN 47403
www.balboapress.com
1 (877) 407-4847

Because of the dynamic nature of the Internet, any web addresses or links contained in this book may have changed since publication and may no longer be valid. The views expressed in this work are solely those of the author and do not necessarily reflect the views of the publisher, and the publisher hereby disclaims any responsibility for them.

The author of this book does not dispense medical advice or prescribe the use of any technique as a form of treatment for physical, emotional, or medical problems without the advice of a physician, either directly or indirectly. The intent of the author is only to offer information of a general nature to help you in your quest for emotional and spiritual well-being. In the event you use any of the information in this book for yourself, which is your constitutional right, the author and the publisher assume no responsibility for your actions.

Any people depicted in stock imagery provided by Thinkstock are models, and such images are being used for illustrative purposes only. Certain stock imagery © Thinkstock.

Print information available on the last page.

ISBN: 978-1-4525-3066-6 (sc)
ISBN: 978-1-4525-3067-3 (e)

Balboa Press rev. date: 09/21/2015

Contents

Foreword

I have watched the evolution and unfolding of this book over several years. It brings into the light the expression of wellbeing, in its broadest sense.

Wholistic wellness encompasses the three aspects of body, mind and spirit. This fundamental concept has guided Tracy on her journey through raising and guiding her family and her study and personal practice of Naturopathy. She has practised this in the way she supports and shares her knowledge with patients, colleagues and friends.

This book represents a culmination of that investment. It is a work of love, a wish to share and an opportunity for us, the readers to use it as a tool in our own journey to understand, achieve and maintain wellness.

Dr Yvonne (Ruby) Bloomfield
M.B.B.S.,D.T.P.M.
General Practitioner
Sydney, Australia

Preface

This book has been an ongoing project now for the last three years. Some weeks it has been in the foreground and others well in the background. The inner prompts to finish and publish kept coming, and so this book is now in your hands.

Wellbeing and health have been an active interest and study of mine for the last 40 years, and I have been fortunate that in the last 20 years I was able to transfer that interest to working in various clinical settings. This journey started from seeking solutions for my own health problems and developed into a deep concern that the discussion about wellbeing is often neglected until you or a family member become seriously sick. At that point, there is no space to consider or discuss the subtle influences of wellbeing because pain and symptom relief are usually the priority. As relief comes and people start feeling better, they are often interested in understanding why they arrived at that point of sickness, how to avoid returning and how to build reserves of wellbeing. They seek a bigger buffer to life's challenges, moving from problem-focused health to awakening wellbeing. Please don't make pain or sickness your prompts to finally care for yourself.

I am grateful for the thousands of conversations I have had with patients around their wellbeing and health. I have been enriched by what I have learnt from their stories. Some people's situations drove me to research more detail about other contributing factors so that I could help them manage their situation better. We all have the same basic needs, but the ratios of what is needed shift as we move through our life stages and challenging environments.

There are reoccurring themes throughout this book of the circular or spiral nature of healing and growth rather than the linear one-directional focus of 'take this and you will be better.' I hope that this book nourishes your heart and mind and stimulates you to look at your wellbeing journey in a new light. What you gain from this book could be different each reading depending on your priorities at the time. It is written in a way so as to help stimulate new insights from within you about your own wellbeing journey. My aim in writing this book is to support you to discover the wonderful, inherent resources you have that support your wellbeing, which can be displayed at any time with sufficient attention and nourishment.

I am grateful to the clinic patients who have patiently waited for 'their reminder book' and practitioners Dr Yvonne Bloomfield, Terry Collinson and Martine Negro in helping with editing and encouragement, and Wendy Millgate for copyediting. Thanks too to my patient family who have enabled it to be finished.

Introduction

When you hear about being well or 'wellbeing' many different ideas and images of what wellbeing means may be conjured up, as you have been exposed to so many advertising images and other information. Allow me to give you a clear, holistic picture of wellbeing and then help you progressively increase your wellbeing every day.

Wellbeing is a process rather than a stationary destination. It is a way of being in order to really experience life fully. To be well is about our capacity to respond to and interact with our social and physical environment with energy and pleasure, each day.

The potential for wellbeing is waiting inside of you all the time. In each moment you can be well. It is always in the present time. The key is to know that it is within you, available abundantly if you *pause* and give it the attention, resources and space it needs to display itself.

Being well requires your co-operation on all three levels of mind, body and spirit in such a way that the needs on each level are being met in a harmonious way. An alternative way of expressing it might be that the survival, emotional, thinking, meaning and seeking parts of you are working together in order for you to enjoy life.

We will be looking at the components and mechanisms of how wellbeing is built and sustained, and how to take in the elements, energy and information you really need. We will be exploring how your mind interacts with your body in a coordinated way through the different parts of your brain, nervous system and hormones in order to experience life. The dynamic friendship between your mind and body sets the first tone of that experience. We will discuss how to restore that friendship if neglect, disappointment and frustration have disrupted it.

The key to your wellbeing is in transforming the quality of the experience of the things you need to do every day. Wellbeing, joy, contentment and happiness can literally be built one breath, step and mouthful of food, conversation or smile at a time.

Wellbeing is not defined by a disease process

Your wellbeing reserves may be challenged by being sick from a cold or having a chronic disease. But the presence of these challenges does not mean that you can't experience wellbeing. Managing them appropriately and developing inner reserves for coping will definitely help you to enjoy wellbeing throughout your whole life.

I know at times having a diagnosis to explain the phenomena someone has been experiencing can be a relief; however, it is extremely important for wellbeing that our identity and wellbeing are not defined by a disease process. For example, it is better to say someone needs to manage their blood sugar levels very consciously than call them a diabetic. Manage them responsibly we must, ignoring them and hoping for the best does not increase our wellbeing.

> '*It's far more important to know what person the disease has than what disease the person has.*' —*Hippocrates*

1

What We Learn from the Beginning of Life

On our search for our 'well-being', understanding the process of the very beginning of our life as a 'human-being' is key. First, let's look at the very beginning of life of a seed that is planted in the ground. Whatever the type of plant, the seed will always send roots downwards through the ground and its stem upwards towards the light. It will vigorously look for the elements it needs and, following its inherent seed information or inner program, it will then process and transform them into itself.

The quality of the seed, the soil, the synchronicity between the local climate and its needs for water and warmth, its ability to access light by whether it's shaded or not, the local insect population and many other factors together will affect the seed and plant's growth and development. If it is vigorous enough it may be able to get past the shade; if not it will be stunted, not reaching its potential, and the same goes if its roots can't spread far. Herein are the clues to what is required for us human beings to grow to completion and full wellness.

What about us humans?

Now let's look more closely at the beginning of your life—the coming together of your unique parcel of information and the universal life energy, in your first environment … your mother. Looking there will reveal some important principles.

Scientists are fast developing a more in-depth understanding of the minute fine tuning of the definite steps in the first three weeks of life. But there is still more to understand. One does get a sense of the respect they have for what they are witnessing. They do know it is orderly and controlled, within tight parameters, through each clear step.

Along its three-day journey through the fallopian tube, from nutrients and genetic instructions contributed by the egg and sperm, the embryo divides to form two cells, then four cells, then eight. At the eight-cell stage, through a process scientists still don't understand, the embryo somehow activates its genes. From this point on, the embryo is on its own to follow its unique genetic destiny. If anything interferes with gene activation, the embryo will die.

As it is entering the uterus it has divided to become sixteen identical cells. In the next 48 hours it will become 100 cells that are two types. The outer ones will become the placenta, which will connect the embryo to the uterus of the mother. The inner ones divide to form the amniotic cavity and a flat disc with two layers of cells that is the embryo.

Once the embryo is embedded in the wall of the uterus, and ensured a supply of oxygen and nutrients from the mother's bloodstream to survive, it starts preparing for a transformation that takes place during the third week of development. The embryo's genes orchestrate, in a very sophisticated process, reconfiguring itself to form three new cell types into inner, middle and outer layers.

Each embryonic cell is now destined to follow a specific developmental pathway. Endoderm cells will go on to form the liver, pancreas and gastrointestinal tract. Cells in the mesoderm develop into the heart and blood vessels, bone, muscle and kidneys. The ectoderm will become the central and peripheral nervous systems, sensory organs, skin and hair.

During this period, the quality of the mother's blood supply is very critical to the long-term health of this new life. Having been activated and cooperating with the environment supplied by its mother and universal life force, this new life grows to emerge nine months later into a new environment.

In this story of all of us who have been born, we can see how there are dynamics at work, which are guided by an intelligent direction to go through each stage. You could say the embryonic cell was following its inner program or template.

The outcome at each stage, however, is influenced by:

- the quality of the supply of nutrients, energy and information

- the embryo's response to this supply and

- other as yet unknown factors from the environmental setting and the embryo's template.

So there is the environment supply, the embryo's information and the relationship between them to produce the outcome. It is also interesting that at one stage at least half of the embryo's resources are allocated to securing its place in its environment via the placenta and the amniotic fluid. The embryo is doing all it can to modify the environment for its survival and development. It is not just passively sitting in it. This dynamic interchange between us, the life forces and our environment continues throughout our life.

Responsive, responsible and balanced

One extra detail is very important to take into account: The environment is divided between the external and the internal environment. In both parts there are things we can see and things we can't. There are things we can influence completely and things that are difficult to influence. We need to be able to take in the elements we require from our internal and external environment and process and transform them into ourselves, and then contribute back into these environments. The more we can acknowledge with respect the universal life energy within us, as well as our unique energy template, the more we will be able to live in a responsive, responsible way towards them as well as our environments.

We may be all in the same physical location, but our experience of it will be very different as we take it into us through our internal environment. The key is whether we are maintaining the delicate balance of the influence of the external environment on our internal environment with our unique energy.

Traditional cultures used to spend a lot of time sharing stories, music and dance to connect with each other for protection and to support each other in processing their daily experiences. In modern culture we seem to have increasingly more external solutions and neglect internal processing and seeking mutual support.

All this requires relationships, and it is the quality of those relationships that determine your level of wellbeing.

The other point to keep in your awareness is how much your cells worked together in the beginning to cooperate with each other and the universal life force ... and this continues throughout your whole life. We may understand some of the inner communications like nerves and hormones, but there are many more that we continue to discover. Your life and wellbeing depend on your relationships, both within and amongst all the different cells and systems at every level of your being. Your life and wellbeing also depends upon your relationships with other people and with the environment.

2

What is Wellbeing and Wellbeing Capacity?

Wellbeing's simplest explanation is having sufficient capacity to meet your needs, combined with a deep level of satisfaction, even in the midst of life's challenges. Satisfaction comes from an engagement with your environment from deep within you, leading also to creativity and joy. Try to think of your wellbeing in terms of making a large container in which peace, vibrancy, contentment, love and joy can be overflowing or radiating from.

Capacity is about having sufficient space to process life in such a way that it gives you energy and nourishment to function and engage in the activities you need and want to do. You have a wellbeing capacity chamber that you are looking after. This container is capable of changing shape and size to accommodate the many challenges that life throws at it, to deliver the outcome of wellbeing. Throughout the rest of this book we will explore the different components of this container as well as highlight the opportunities you have to impact the quality of each one. You will find certain concepts mentioned again in different contexts. This is because there is much interweaving of the various influences on our wellbeing and looking at the same component from a different angle will show more clearly that sometimes it's in the driver seat setting the agenda and sometimes it's being influenced more by other factors.

For example, you can look at stress and your nutrition levels from at least two different perspectives. You may feel stressed because you don't have the nourishment you need to function properly, and as soon as your nutrient levels are restored you feel well as you adapt more easily to the stressors. Or maybe on paper you should be having sufficient nutrition in your diet, but you may not be digesting food properly because of stress. Perhaps your enzyme-making inheritance makes certain foods difficult to digest and thus you are not absorbing the full amount you need from your food. It will be a journey to connect with your digestive capacity's response to stress and what foods and situations for eating suits you best to have the level of nutrients you need.

Space

The simple concept of space is profound in its implication of how we deal with everything. If I asked you to sort out a box of distinctly different files on your lap, you would find that a much more frustrating experience than if you had a big table that you could spread everything out on in clear piles. If I asked you to do it in 30 minutes, it would be more stressful than if you had 2 hours. If I made you listen to jack hammer noise rather than music you enjoyed, it would be harder.

Imagine that you do have the time, space or room to spread out and see things clearly...

You have the time and space to take it slow and have moments to pause and think about what you are doing...

You have the space of not having an annoying sound in the background disturbing your focus...

The same quantity of water in a cup may fill it to the brim and be easily spilt, but in a bigger container it is easily managed. The same task becomes a completely different experience.

You may ask, 'Where am I going to find extra time or space?' The answer lies in learning how to reset the imbalance of resource sharing within your systems, relaxing the tension in your body and changing the quality of activities you have to do.

> *Practise kindness and gratitude—you can be*
> *filled with them and still have space for life.*

Collaborative relationships

Central to your wellbeing is to establish collaborative relationships between all the different systems of organisation and function within your body as well as within your social and physical environment. Collaboration includes respectful co-operation, integration—the bringing together of separate different but interconnected energies and processes via feedback and communication mechanisms, harmony and rhythm. This is a method or way as well as a goal.

Humans process our experiences through combining our rational and creative intelligence with the innate qualities we possess that are similar or the same as minerals, plants and animals. That is, our primal instinct for survival is combined with the social need for connection, pleasure and meaning—from being part of something bigger than ourselves—and our creative, imaginative impulses.

We have within us energy and information processing systems of immense sophistication and capability. The more they are nourished and enabled to work together smoothly the greater your wellbeing.

The way geographers describe ecosystems and the whole planet biosphere could easily be transferred to us. We have a digestive system, immune system, circulatory system, nervous system and so on with complex feedback and organisational processes. They have various responsibilities to keep us both surviving and thriving. Many activities continue without our continual conscious input, on autopilot from the combination of our unique blueprint plus our accumulated associations and memories. These activities as demonstrated by biofeedback can be further refined by our growing awareness and consciousness.

Your wellbeing outflows, or radiates, from within your core wellbeing chamber. It feeds into your satisfaction and supports your structure and function. This is analogous to how music can be considered an outflow from an orchestra or band. The quality of the music comes from many components. The talent and capability of each musician, the quality and type of their instruments as well as their ability to harmonise together all contribute to the sound.

This also leads us to the subjective nature of evaluating our wellbeing. An analogy might be in our choice of music; whether it suits our taste or not influences our enjoyment of the music. Incompetent musicians, as well, can hinder the enjoyment of a song normally enjoyed, while good musicians can make many types of music more pleasurable. At any point in your life, whether the needs around your personal priorities, expectations and perspectives can be met, will impact your feeling of wellbeing.

Wellbeing is not about everything being perfect. Although we try to seek the best way we can to avoid or manage sickness or injuries, through the 'perfect' diet or exercise program, things will happen. So it's important to invest in your ability to cope and recover from life's challenges, digest the experiences, and grow in both wisdom and empathy.

Your unique pattern

Critical to your wellbeing is your capacity to stay aligned with your unique pattern of potential growth and development, while interacting with your environment in both a responsive and influencing way. Your unique pattern comes from two family histories coming together plus more. Your unique pattern is part of a bigger pattern.

Australian Aboriginal art, which deeply demonstrates this, has been embraced as an awakening to our connectedness to everyone and everything. Every stroke and dot is significant in the whole picture. We have a greater significance than any of us truly realise. Being the best you, developing yourself and contributing who you are, is really important. Every one of us matters in the human race, as we carry something unique and special that makes us all richer. Honouring who you are as well as honouring those around you is a very important aspect of wellbeing, and this includes our global wellbeing.

> *There is a delicate balance between serving attentively the needs of others as well as ourselves, and we must attend to both.*

Circles of care

In nature we can see many circles and spirals. They are not only beautiful but geometrically and mathematically they enable stable, sustainable structure, function, growth and development. For example, the oceans circle the globe and rhythmically lap at the earth's edges.

When we breathe we make a circle with the air coming into us and going out. This is a vital cycle for our life, and all of our systems benefit when this happens rhythmically and smoothly. There are whole books just on this subject and powerful therapies helping people to achieve freer breathing. There is an inner circle between us and our environment, but we have many other inner and outer ones. We will discuss this more in *Chapter 6 Live with Rhythm*.

We all have a value of one (1), with every being in relationship with every other being. So we love and care for ourselves as well as others. It's not about caring for others and not yourself, or the other way around; that is, caring for yourself and not others. It's about both together—then it is sustainable.

The ultimate circle is the one where we go inside and discover who we are, bring ourselves out into our environment, and then bring more into ourselves from the environment to allow more of ourselves to be expressed collaboratively and comfortably. To raise the quality of your caring, circulate your attention with listening, scanning, and connecting to yourself and your environment to check if anything needs adjusting or attending to with more actions.

Care stands for:

Consistent

Attention

Refreshes

Everything

How to increase your wellbeing capacity

We have touched on several elements necessary for building your wellness capacity, such as space and collaboration. In the following chapters we will explore the necessary components, resources, processing and allocation required to build your capacity for wellness. Your wellness capacity foundation components are:

- Space: sufficient time and a feeling of spaciousness, inside and out, from a lack of congestion. This reflects your reserves and the free and appropriate allocation of resources for adaption.

- connections with others and your environment

- regular renewing and repairing from having adequate resources and a balanced nervous system

- sufficient supply of the resources, energy and information needed for structure, function and satisfaction by:

- gathering the elements or nourishment you need

- managing the transition zones and processing

- allocating resources appropriately

- clearing waste away efficiently

The following chapters will help you actively enhance your ability to do these fundamentals well. All the ensuing suggestions feed into each other and combine to build a momentum towards reaching a tipping point in creating a perfect size container, one where wellbeing becomes easy to sustain. Leaving out one part can put a greater strain on building the momentum and is therefore harder to sustain.

3

Gathering Your Nourishing Resources

We need nourishment for mind, body and spirit. The main resources or elements needed to generate your energy and information exchange requirements are sourced from good quality food and water, quality air, light, music, inspiring words, time in nature and a supportive environment where we have happy human relationships based on positive connection with others. Last but not least is cooperation with our inner self. If we are dealing with environments either inside or outside of ourselves that include greater toxicity then the need of certain nutrients increases.

One of the main ways we take in nutrients is through food and water. Our body is at least 75 per cent water, and water is involved in many chemical processes of the body. So our body needs fresh water every day. It also has to maintain an acid/alkaline balance, which is tightly controlled. A simple carbon water filter, which you change at the appropriate intervals, improves the taste of plain water, thus enabling you to avoid water from plastic bottles or adding flavourings, or drinking sodas, excessive fruit juices, teas or coffees. If you need to talk a lot for work, or work in an air conditioned environment, you can lose a large amount of moisture. If not replaced, dehydration becomes a stress trigger to your body. Some people misread the signal for thirst as a signal for hunger or stimulation. Various minerals are needed for the acid/alkaline balance and they also provide structure and function. Protein is necessary for your muscles to do work and also to provide the raw materials needed for various communications, immune and repair functions of the body, like enzymes, neurotransmitters, immune system components and many hormones. A range of vitamins are essential to enable these enzymes to work effectively.

The body controls our blood sugar levels to be at a steady rate to power the work of the cells. The subtle minerals and vitamins within the food and water we ingest combine with oxygen to release glucose from our food or the body's energy store sites. So-called 'energy' drinks, full of sugar, are not needed.

Food choices

For optimum health, half of your food needs to come from a wide variety of vegetables, especially green leafy ones. Fresh is best, organic if possible, with the addition of some naturally fermented ones.

Green leafy vegetables not only provide carbohydrates for energy but vital minerals, macro and micro (including calcium) as well as omega-3 essential fatty acids, phytochemicals and antioxidants. Although wild gorillas are not known to develop obesity or heart disease, captive gorillas fed processed but nutritious biscuits are just as susceptible to these conditions as humans. The Cleveland Zoo recently showed that returning its gorillas to a diet rich in leafy greens caused them to lose excess weight.

A small area of fresh greens growing in healthy soil in your yard, or even inside in a little pot, is a great investment for your health. It's very satisfying to pick the leaves you need for that day or meal, and you get the peak nutrition.

Fresh whole fruit also provides a great abundance of nutrients, but it is very important to be careful to not overload with sugars from eating too much sweet fruit.

Sprouted legumes consumed raw or cooked, **nuts**, **seeds**, **eggs**, **fish**, **meat** and **poultry** complete the essential proteins, fatty acids, carbohydrates, minerals and vitamins your body needs.

For those who have extra energy needs to play sport or do manual labour a selection from a broad range of **whole grains** like brown and wild rice, millet, quinoa, barley, sorghum, buck wheat, oats, amaranth and wheat will give you the extra energy and B vitamins you need to release them. Processed 'white' grains take B vitamins from your body to process and spike your blood sugar, causing other problems. Be careful of modern wheat; it is different to what was available even fifty years ago, causing some to feel more easily bloated and elevating their blood sugar too quickly. Many people are surprised how much better they feel from just leaving wheat out of their diet and giving their bodies a rest from it.

To go into the details of the proportions you personally need are beyond the purpose of this book. One thing to remember, though, is that your stomach size is about the size of your two hands cupped together. You don't want to put more than that in at a time, including liquids, if you want it to do its job properly.

I think I will serve you better in calling your attention to certain aspects of nutrition you may not have considered before, which I have personally experienced as well as in my clinical practice, rather than asserting another 'perfect diet'. Even though I have been interested in and studied nutrition for forty years, I know it is not just about the vitamins, minerals, calorie, protein and oils count. Initially, I, like most, thought it would be that simple!

Mostly we can receive sufficient nourishment from eating a wide variety of well-balanced food sources. However, it is good to bear in mind that soils can be low in certain minerals like zinc or sulphur. Ensuring supplementation or consciously eating more of some food items becomes critical if you are to give the body the range of nutrients it needs. Australian soils, being an old land, are particularly vulnerable.

Of course, if you fill up on steamed vegetables, rather than cakes and processed food, you will certainly maintain pain-free and healthy living for longer! It is also one thing to share a slice of a birthday cake and another to be buying cake for yourself each day. One of the problems of modern consumerism is that foods that were once only for special occasions have now become an everyday 'food' and have pushed out of the diet truly nourishing food. Sometimes we are looking for some other kind of comfort for our soul and use food instead. It is a good idea to put into your life ways of nourishing your mind and heart first to make it easier to not eat certain damaging foods as often. Think about what experience or feeling you are trying to recreate in your life through that food and work with it. Substituting other things, having it less frequently or having a smaller portion, eaten mindfully, are better options.

As a general guide it is better to eat a good breakfast every morning and consume foods requiring greater digestion before 7 pm. This enables our eating pattern to be more in sync with the digestive system's needs and abilities.

Fermented foods

An important part of nourishment is naturally fermented food. Historically, fermented foods have played an important role in the diets of almost every society throughout the world. Fermentation is a method of food preservation that also enhances the nutrient content. The action of the Lactobacillus bacteria makes the minerals in fermented or 'cultured' food more readily available to the body. The bacteria also produce B vitamins, essential fatty acids and enzymes that are beneficial for digestion. Preparing different vegetables to sit within a brine solution is all that is needed. The addition of a starter can speed up the process. There are many simple methods and great recipes readily available in books and on the internet. It is important that they are made authentically and not manufactured to be taste equivalent.

One of the key features of the famous Mediterranean diet is the use of garlic and flavouring herbs like thyme and oregano. These foods also selectively target unhelpful bacteria in the digestive tract, explaining another reason for the diet's anti-inflammatory effect.

Avoid toxicity and read labels carefully. Be careful of ingesting toxicity. Pure air, water and food are an essential start. Your body requires more resources to process polluted or contaminated air, water and food than unadulterated. Flavour enhancers, preservatives, colouring, thickeners and sweeteners can easily overload your detoxing system over time. If manufacturers do test the impact of a chemical on the body, it is one at a time and not the mix that is actually consumed in many drinks or processed foods, even if they have the big words 'fat free', 'gluten free' or 'cholesterol free' on the package.

For the times that you do buy processed food, please do read the labels carefully! Avoid low fat options as the extra sugar and chemicals added to give the impression to your taste buds of creaminess are more fattening, once within the body, than the fat that was taken out. Remember, it's not the large print attracting your attention that is necessarily the main ingredient. Look for what is listed first or the percentage value depending on which country you live in. Also be watchful of your personal care and household cleaning products that may increase your toxic load.

Environment for eating

The next thing after food choices is the environment in which you eat and how you eat to ensure you can digest and absorb your food well. For example, eat in a relaxed comfortable environment. The evening news or certain other forms of 'entertainment' and eating a meal do not mix well. If what you are listening to is upsetting or exciting then your autonomic nervous system becomes responsive to that disturbance and allocates less energy to digestion as it feels it needs to defend you from something. Pausing and looking at your food and taking in its aroma, with gratitude, helps prepare your digestive organs (stomach, pancreas and liver) to process the food better. Eating slowly and chewing your food well also assists as good digestion starts in the mouth, with the saliva's digestive enzymes.

Food is a connector

Food is not only critical for nutrition but is also a fundamental way we connect with each other. After breathing food is the first thing we look for to connect and bond with our mother. Just as within the womb we associated safety with our mother's heartbeat, nestling at the breast for a good drink of milk right next to the heart is very reassuring. So food is a comfort to us.

Our community, family and individual culture around food is very important to also consider. We can have a very strong internal response to some foods, not just from their chemical components, colour and smell but also from their associated memories. I know one lady who gets a rash on her leg if she eats certain foods by herself at home but not if she eats the same ones in the company of others. She has happy memories eating with a large family as a child, which modifies her experience.

This inheritance we have is not just in our genes but in our family pattern, culture and stories around food, as well as in their nutritional status at certain times in the family history. For example, consider the situation of your maternal grandmother when she was pregnant with your mother as well your mother's situation when pregnant with you as part of your inheritance. That situation includes their nutritional status, overall health and stress levels.

Acknowledging these other components in your eating experience helps you to pinpoint why you may be eating something and to ask yourself, "Do I want to continue this pattern I inherited or learnt, or do I want to make a new one that serves me better now".

Music and nature

Music that you enjoy is a really important part of nourishing yourself. It is good for you on every level, helping to process life, especially the emotional aspects, change your mood, relieve your stress response, and bring joy and energy into your life. It also connects us to the rhythm of life. More on that in Chapter 6.

Time in nature, enjoying natural sunlight and fresh air, is also very restorative. Natural sunlight is an important regulator of our rhythm. Sufficient safe skin exposure helps us to create vitamin D, which is important for bone health as well as cell differentiation.

Fresh air is a fundamental need. Every cell needs oxygen to meet its energy needs. Air pollution is the single biggest environmental health risk, according to WHO in March 2014, being a contributing factor in vascular as well as lung health. Breathing not only brings in oxygen but also the release of carbon dioxide, which is an important aspect of the acid/alkaline balance.

Time in nature not only brings us more sunlight and oxygen, it reminds us of our roots, teaches us, inspires us and is an important way to recharge our own electromagnetic energy. Just walking quietly or sitting in the bush, a forest or a park or besides the ocean or river on a regular basis will make a significant difference to your wellbeing. We may not know all the mechanisms or reasons, but you know that you will feel more relaxed and more cheery, with a broader perspective on aspects of your life.

Inspiring words

Inspiring words help us to have hope, vision, comfort and reassurance.

They neutralise negativity and destructive words.

They encourage us and guide us to navigate difficulties or obstacles in our path.

They help us to learn from others, possibly reducing having to go through every personal lesson painfully.

They have many sources for example in books, lyrics in songs, movie lines and conversations.

Connections with others and self

Open friendly time with others is an integral part of being human. We need each other for safety, pleasure and meaning. In past ages social isolation could threaten your survival because of the harshness of the environment. The delicate balance of the sympathetic and parasympathetic branches of the autonomic nervous systems, which will be discussed in allocation of resources in Chapter 4, is hard wired to your giving and receiving appropriate facial signal cues. Our 'space' is linked to the quality of these relationships.

Honest searching, reflecting and honouring your highest self expand you. There is more potential in you than you will probably have time to develop in your lifetime, but why not keep exploring and sharing? Being at peace with your heart and conscience as well as your survival instincts is critical for your wellbeing.

4

Processing in Transition Zones and Resource Allocation

For resources to be fully utilised by us, they have to pass through processing within our body's inner transition zones. We have complex structures and processing centres to manage the borders between our environment and ourselves. Two examples are the lungs and the digestive system. Superficially it may seem they are just processing air, food and water, which is a big essential job in itself. However, have you had the experience of being aware that when you feel certain emotions your breathing or digestive tract constricts or you feel 'butterflies in your tummy'? These two areas in your body may feel very different before or after giving a public speech! These are the two areas most braced to deal with difficult 'news'.

The whole digestive tract from mouth to anus is a processing centre. And it is not only the digestive system working; every other system is involved in support, especially the immune and nervous systems. Trillions of bacteria are involved in supporting the immune system while also providing certain nutrients to your body. The digestive system is not only dealing with the food you have presented to it but also the simultaneous information coming in from your other senses. Then there is a dynamic information flow between other processing centres in the brain and heart. Sometimes there is no room for the food you have eaten as the other information is so intense; many times the food will get blamed.

There are many sources of this other information:

- what you were doing before eating

- the cook's thinking and feeling about cooking

- the physical environment you are eating in

- the social environment

- any old memories about the location or food.

Emotional and mental processing

To take in the energy and information to nourish your heart and mind you also need to process and digest your life experience.

The gaining of wisdom is not automatic, and parts of your life may stay 'undigested', packed in storage.

The hopeful news is that you can learn to acknowledge and release life challenges, to allow fresh opportunities for lessons and joy to enter your life.

I am still taken by surprise about some things that come out of my cell memory or 'storage' then out of my mouth or later out of my bowels, which I know are not from what I have been eating but what I was talking about! So I have learned the skill to acknowledge my experience and contain, if necessary, my indigestion of certain situations or feelings so they don't disturb my relationships with other people.

You may eat the ideal organic diet for your genetic inheritance, in wonderful settings, chewing and savouring each mouthful, and you would still have to go to the toilet. This is the nature of life with its cyclic rhythm. There are waste products produced from every cell, as well as left-over fibre from digestion, which acts as a broom to move the other waste out of the body. Your lungs, kidneys, liver and skin are doing their best to get rid of waste all the time. If they get overloaded, the body dumps them into fat cells or they form little pockets in the gut.

In the same way, you could have what some would call the ideal life: good health, loving family and friends, pleasant surroundings, financial security; but you still need to process your experiences to gain wisdom and empathy, and to let go of any unhelpful emotions and make room for the next stage of life.

To be really satisfied there needs to be good 'life digestion'
that is nourishing your inner template for it to emerge.

Breathing

Breathing not only feeds into the processing of air, for oxygen and balancing of our acid/alkaline needs, but the nervous system changes the pace and rhythm of breathing when there is danger to deal with or you are processing many emotions. Deepening your breathing to expand your belly area and slowing breathing can help you to become calm and steady.

In a process of awareness development you can learn to accurately discern, through observing your breathing, what you are really feeling, what is actually happening and how much of your previously associated memories, filters and perspective are assisting or hindering you to deal with the present moment.

Allocation of resources

Having sufficient energy in the transition zones to enable processing or digestion is dependent upon the overall allocation of resources by the autonomic nervous system. Your overall capacity may be greater than what you are feeling in any moment because of the allocation of resources by the brain and nervous system. Remember how much of the embryo's resources in the womb were allocated to survival? It is at least half. This continues on throughout life, even though you may not be consciously thinking about survival and safety. You might be thinking, *Oh I have to put up with this unpleasant part of my job to pay my bills* or *I need to eat and drink some water before I wilt* and so on. Your body's inner intelligence is monitoring very closely the parameters it needs to maintain so that your body can host the universal life force! The body has a hunger for survival and balance. It is seeking to defend you as well as tightly manage the oxygen, acid/alkaline balance, hydration, temperature, blood glucose and repair parameters. The body prompts you to do things to help manage survival and health. It has a space within the nerve/hormonal mechanisms for your conscious response and feedback to its signals, to adjust your immediate experience. This is an important way our awareness and consequent decisions influence our neurocircuitry of nerves, muscles and hormones.

Let's explore some scenarios:

1. You are busy working on a project and you notice you are slightly shivering. You have been so focused you didn't notice the temperature dropped, but your body did and started doing something automatically. What does your conscious self do with that information? There is some space in the processing loops of the brain for your choices and what you do now will have different outcomes. You could respond promptly and either put more clothes on, change the air-conditioning or turn a heater on and after a short while your body is comfortable again. You could ignore the feeling and go back to your work, dismissing it or internally saying to your body, *Sorry, I'll do something when I finished this next point*, which you do and once again your body settles. What if you keep ignoring the signals? Your body may become so cold that it's starting to put a lot of resources in keeping warm and now you are starting to feel uncomfortable in the throat or sinuses. The body knows that you

can't always respond immediately, and it does its best to adjust. But the subtle difference between not acknowledging the information consistently means that a gap develops within and you become more and more disconnected from your own body. Athletes show us we can train and modify the body's responses over time. Athletes also show that if you just override its signals in an imbalanced way, you can take longer to recover from injury and illness.

2. You start feeling a bit fuzzy in the head, a bit agitated. Actually, your body is now thirsty. Do you recognise the signals and give it some fresh water, and therefore feel refreshed, or do you ignore it? Do you think you need a stimulant like coffee to clear your fuzziness, which makes your body feel more dehydrated and now frustrated because you are not responding to its signals appropriately? If you have some sort of sugary drink, either soft drink or even concentrated fruit juice, you send your body through another energy roller coaster, when all it needed was fresh water.

3. Your body puts the highest priority on keeping you safe. Within the defence role anything that is *perceived* as being of immediate danger, for instance defending you from a lion that may eat you at any minute, is given priority over fighting a virus that is dangerous but not immediate. Digestion and repair are postponed in the face of immediate danger. This tendency of the body is perfect for the short term. In the long term, however, this continual lack of attending to everyday maintenance can cause problems.

Did you notice that I highlighted *perceived* above. The information received from your senses is linked in with your perspective to gauge for danger. Your nervous system and hormones will be activated quickly, assuming you are correct, but are willing to be modified afterwards if your initial interpretation was not correct, or to be reassured the danger has passed. For instance, your body prefers you to start running, if you glance at something that looks like a snake, get to safety and then realise it is a garden hose than assume it is a garden hose and casually go to pick it up and it is a snake that bites you! In modern life you may perceive vicious 'lions' and 'snakes' in many situations, depending on your memories, posture, beliefs or stories you have heard, read or watched, and this may happen a hundred times a day. The more you don't recognize these reactions happening in your nervous system and adjust your approach the less energy you will have. The more you do notice adjust yourself the more energy energized you will feel, even doing the same activities.

Light-hearted, comfortable relationships with those you live and work with every day is a vital trigger for your body to feel safe. Our individual capacity to cope with stress is greatly enhanced when we are connected to a team, which is also a part of a bigger team. Social isolation diminishes our capacity for our renewal and repair systems to have the time and resources they need to do their jobs. Yes, we all need to have time alone to reflect and regroup in varying amounts, but this is different in feeling from being socially isolated.

The mind and body dynamic

The mind and body have a dynamic, interconnected, interdependent relationship, with a two-way directional influence on each other. You may notice this when you watch a movie. Your body will go through all sorts of sensations as you are influenced by the various emotions that have been stimulated by the movie. Certainly advertisers know how to stimulate changes within us, associated with their product. Awareness of what you are thinking and how you are using your body can help maintain a neutral physical posture that is less taxing for the body and allows more openness for the mind.

The central and peripheral nervous systems, which are the instruments of this dynamic, are composed of the brain, spinal cord, sympathetic, parasympathetic and enteric nervous systems. Many parts are working automatically, constantly controlling the body's response to environmental changes, whether you are awake or asleep, thinking about it consciously or not. They work cooperatively and independently, with some areas focused on your survival and others on your learning and growing. That's why on one hand we can be excited about something but on the other have a feeling of butterflies in the stomach, or worse. This is also why we can have an inspiration or insightful understanding for a new way of doing something, say playing a musical instrument, but to implement it means you have to practice to get through all the layers of neuron memory and entanglement to make new neuron connections between your brain and muscles to embody that idea.

Within the brain there are complex structures working to fine tune the adjustments of resources needed by the body to deal with defence, maintenance of the normal internal environment of the body (temperature, salt concentration, blood sugar, oxygen and carbon dioxide level in blood and so on), learning and creativity for you to enjoy life. They pass to and receive messages from the endocrine system, heart, blood vessels and other visceral organs.

Imminent danger defence takes the highest priority. The sympathetic nervous system changes gears from keeping you awake and engaged with your environment to preparing to fight or flee—unless it gets counter signals very quickly. In some incidents it works in micro seconds. The parasympathetic nervous system of relaxation and repair is reduced accordingly as the sympathetic goes up.

The parasympathetic nervous system of facial expression communications will not be used in the case of a lion but may be used with other animals or people if that can mean avoiding fighting or fleeing. This is abandoned if the danger is not decreasing quickly. Resources are sent to the large muscle limbs, mobilising circulation and glucose systems to participate through hormonal and nerve activity. It prepares the body to put out energy and to protect it from any effects of injury. It shunts resources or circulation from the gut and bone marrow, speeds up the heart, increases blood pressure, dilates the pupils of the eyes and makes more glucose available in the blood for energy.

Many people are aware of the 'flight or fight' response. You may experience it as a startle, a more shallow breath, and a bracing or tightening of especially your belly and calf muscles. This response is critical in allocating resources depending on whether there is danger or not. Significantly, it can be connected to physical danger or from social isolation, because that has been so critical to our ancestors' survival. Either fighting, fleeing or connecting with a "safe" person can resolve the stress. If neither is possible or successful, the sympathetic arousal can get so extreme that it is too much for the body to handle. At this point, the parasympathetic system wrenches up its gears for your survival. It comes in so strongly that it overwhelms the sympathetic arousal and sends the person into a state of immobilisation. There is an extreme shut down of metabolic functions resulting in very low heart rate and blood pressure, a release of opioids to numb pain, and at a psychological level, dissociation of awareness. This can be full collapse, dissociation, or a more partial freeze such as an inability to think clearly, access words or emotions or move parts of the body. This can be momentary such as a possum freezing and becoming reanimated after the predator leaves.

However, in humans it can continue indefinitely and most commonly occurs in trauma and shame, which is developmental trauma. Support from others is critical to enable resolution and continued development of constructive integrated neuropathways. Social experiences can move from defensive awkwardness around certain subjects or people to a relaxed comfortableness over time.

These autonomic up-gearing and down-regulating reconfigurations are responding to both the internal environment of our thoughts and feelings as well as the external environment. The heart and digestive systems respond to the facial features of others through the vagus nerves. Digestion is influenced by the people we are eating with! Muscles get involved as we think—as any athlete will tell you. Why do some athletes perform better in training than in competition and for others it is the reverse?

We are programmed to have this reflex response to danger because if there was, for example a lion or pack of wolves, we may not have time to think how to respond. However, we are also meant to deconstruct our experiences, take in information from the whole body to learn the lessons, so we can avoid future danger. There is supposed to be a two-way dialogue about your experience of life between your mind and body, so you can learn and adapt to do better. When you notice you have braced, it doesn't help to ignore it. We all must learn more about both the internal environment of ourselves and the external that is leading to the tension, otherwise we can live under the extreme sympathetic/parasympathetic reactivity adjustments, which is very wearing.

This shunting between fight/flight/freeze takes tremendous resources away from the regular maintenance of temperature, glucose, acid/alkaline and so on as well as repair. Instead of having an easy flow between sympathetic and parasympathetic systems hundreds of times throughout the day, like our two legs in walking, these systems may be both geared up to emergency mode in a disjointed arrangement, in a state of conflict instead of cooperation. Therefore, little things become hard to do. It is like shifting from driving at normal speed using the accelerator and brake as appropriate, to driving quickly and using the handbrake. The 'space' for thinking has been taken over by freezing and unfreezing, trying to process what is happening. Space for processing helps us to reset, untangle and complete homeostasis and balanced responsiveness. In *Chapter 5 Skills to Practise for a Well Life* we will explore ways to reclaim your 'space'.

Gut microflora

As another aspect of this story of conflict or fight/flight/ freeze above is that the type of gut bacteria we have become extra significant in helping the immune system, which may not be receiving backups from the bone marrow. You may recall that resources are shunted from digestion and bone marrow in times of stress. Researchers are now discovering how much the bacteria in our gut communicate with our neurons and immune system and can be either an important back-up system or an opportunistic catastrophe.

Good bacteria help protect us from other pathogens as well as provide B and K vitamins and fatty acids. The epithelial cells of the gut need to be replaced every 3 to 5 days as it is such a harsh environment. So the nourishment provided by the bacteria is very helpful; at times it is critical.

On the other hand, inappropriate bacteria can be more damaging to the cells and create extra burden on the immune system. They send signals to your nervous system, trying to trick it to create the environment beneficial to them but not necessarily you! In particular, they like sweet conditions. In British research bacteria stimulated cravings for certain chocolate!

Naturally fermented vegetables and garlic help provide the best environment in the gut to support the good bacteria. Sugary foods, lack of fibre and antibiotics compromise it.

Too much bracing from stress can also interfere with the smooth functioning of the ileocecal valve between the small and large intestine. This valve is influenced by the natural movement of the intestine, nerves and our hormones. If it goes into spasm and is not shut fully or responds appropriately, the location of bacteria in our gut is influenced. Some bacteria are okay for us in one part of the gut and not the other. This valve can be helped to relax and function better by placing your hand just to the left of your right hip. The warmth of your hand, even for a minute, helps.

Thoughts influence nerves

The autonomic nervous system responds to our thoughts. It can't know if you have heard or seen a real lion or something or someone you feel is a lion—it just goes off. Depending on the thoughts and scenarios that you keep mulling over in your mind, they can send signals from the brain charged with electricity and emotion to your autonomic nervous system, which releases a whole cascade of hormones and other chemicals. If this is a good scene with pleasant images, your autonomic nervous system is going to allocate resources and signals to relaxation, social engagement, digestion, detoxifying, internal immune system, repair, renewal and sleep. If on the other hand it is a scenario that is frightening, dangerous or promoting feelings of anger, your resources are reallocated throughout your body, increasing your blood pressure, heart rate and blood glucose levels so that you are prepared for action to fight or flee or for a parasympathetic freeze if your survival mechanisms thinks that is the best protection for you. When this vigilance of the nervous system is activated, you might feel as though you are on the spectrum of anxiety. If this continues too long, a mechanism that is good for quick action can become tired and your digestive system, immune system and sleep patterns become impaired.

Applying your 'pause and breathe slowly skills'
help reset your nervous system immediately.
Your autonomic nerves live in the now.

The limbic part of the brain is one centre of emotional activity that is being researched more. It receives stimulus from our concepts and mental mulling and from our primal survival gut feelings. Our emotions are there to give us the energy to create or do, so powerful waves of energy stimulate hormones and our nerves to take action. If you can't or don't, because it is socially inappropriate, your body is left to process chemicals in the liver and kidney and excess electrical energy needs to be discharged. It takes extra energy and activation of other muscles to restrain these action impulses. This can lead to muscle tightness or 'knots of muscle pain' and physical and emotional fatigue.

On the other hand, when you are feeling discouraged or disappointed and find that you are slumped in your body a certain way, by adjusting your body or walking a short distance your mood can lift as your body is sending signals back up through the limbic system to the rest of your brain, and your thinking can become clearer. Your nervous system releases its previous pattern as you have given it the feedback it needs to complete the previous cycle. It wants to be able to move away from alert danger mode too!

We can learn to sift our thoughts and recognise they come from many sources. We can't choose many of the thoughts that pop up, but we can choose the ones we mull over and put weight on.

Emotions

Emotions enrich life and empower us to take action. There are no good or bad emotions. There are some that are more contextually appropriate or that we need to make more room for. There may be some that linger on too long and thus throw out the balance or appropriate proportions of our emotional experience. Emotions come from many sources and they are an integral driver of the allocation of resources.

Our emotional response to our environment is a combination of:

- sensory information

- sensations in our body

- the story we are telling ourselves to give emotional meaning to experiences

- memory of events in the past

- anticipation and expectation of the future

- the way you hold your body.

Adapting or coping?

The body does have reserves to cope with adaption. These reserves and adaptive capacity differ from person to person. There are adaptions which happen with growth because we have learnt how to deal with our environment better, and on the other hand there is adaption because the body has no choice and it copes. The former adaption indicates a harmony between our instinctive, social and rational parts of us. The latter will hit a limitation as the body cannot continually adapt without exhaustion. Adaptive herbs and nutrients can help, but for the long term a change of behaviour or environment must occur or there will be a collapse of the weakest system in the body.

The body's way to cope with smoking

When someone first smokes they cough as the reflex of the body to rid itself of irritants kicks in. Some people stop then, and others continue. The body still wants to rid itself of the toxins, but it adopts other methods and the cough disappears for a while. Later on, if the person continues to smoke, they will start coughing all the time as the body has exhausted its capacity to cope with the irritations in other ways. At any time up to this point, if the person stops smoking, the body immediately starts the road back to its original pattern, away from the pattern it had to adopt because of the cigarettes.

If you are an adaptive person then you have been able to navigate well through your environmental influences. You can respond in a way to life that enables you to learn what works and what doesn't and apply it to the future.

By practising attentive engagement and writing your observations weekly about your life, you 'work the soil' for even previously entrenched habits to become looser and lighter to work with. They will no longer have the same power over you as you slowly build up the skills for pulling them out of your life. There is no substance, natural or pharmaceutical, that can replace or fill the little gap there is in your feedback circuitry for conscious participation in your learning, growth and self-care.

Bracing is a way we may react to stress; however, it is important to release this 'coping' mechanism as it can lead to breathing problems and indigestion. It can also disrupt the ileocecal valve function, which can disturb bacteria distribution in the gut, technically called 'dysbiosis'. The best way to release this unhelpful pattern is to regularly, throughout the day, slowly breathe out and pull in your belly button towards your spine to expel the last bit of air, and then let the air fill your belly area naturally. Once again breathe out slowly as if you were cooling soup on a spoon and pull your belly towards your spine. By repeating this exercise three times you will find it helps to reset the calm balance of the nervous system and enable pleasurable responsiveness, even to challenges. It is pleasurable because a part of you knows that when you meet a challenge, you grow and learn.

Carefully avoid relying on the body's short-term coping strategies for the long term. Coping strategies are very energy expensive and strain the body. Some people have greater reserves than others from their inherited constitutions, but there are limits to delaying repair and renewal of immune and enzyme reserves.

Physical and emotional injuries

Prolonged recovery from physical or emotional injury takes extra resources every day to carry. Physical injury requires a balance between sufficient rest, correct treatment and exercises to help the area fully recover and be reconnected with you as a whole.

It is vital that emotional injury is not buried and ignored, nor takes over your life. It needs to be protected and contained while you are processing and healing so there is no opportunity for manipulation by bullies or disturbing of your own perception. At the same time, it is important to be careful that you don't adopt an overall over-protectiveness of yourself. For example, as you process feeling very embarrassed by a teacher you can move through reactivity to all authority figures to a specific teacher under specific circumstances that you will be better prepared for. As well, you can learn how to recover more quickly if you do feel embarrassed. This is better than feeling over-protected and afraid or aggressive in a setting with someone who triggers that unconscious, embarrassed memory within you.

Fear which you experience during a car accident may somatise in the body, that is. the experience becomes trapped in cellular memory. While the accident may hurt physically, the emotional ramifications may go unnoticed. Thus the physical pain overshadows the feeling of fear that runs through our body at the same time.

Physical therapy would take care of the painful condition of the injury; however, the psychological shock will settle within the body, possibly taking shape in the tensed muscles of the chest, jaws or back, or may be layered over previous physical or emotional traumas. Therefore, the psychological shock may, for example, pull the stressed muscles of the spine or other joints out of alignment.

The body and mind become frozen or crystallised around the emotions and psychological shock. When the emotions remain unprocessed, they take extra resources from the body in order to be contained -resources which are needed for the body's various systems, to be maintained properly. Your body/mind system uses these 'crystallised' emotions as a bookmark, hopeful that at some point in time you will read the message and learn the lesson that you were not able learn or understand at the time of the trauma. This is so that you will learn from experience and not repeat it. The neurons want to fulfil their purpose in giving you that information.

I am grateful for the research of Dr Stephen Porges, Dr Peter Levine as well as other stress and trauma researchers and clinicians, to help us understand what I have observed in my patients and own life journeys. Recognising the impact of my childhood stress pattern on my digestive system, slowly releasing the pattern and making new supportive habits —was life changing for me.

Clearing waste products

Your body has many waste disposal systems. Even with the most ideal diet and life there are metabolic waste products that need to be cleared. However, modern life's new combinations of chemicals, leading to air, water and food contamination, can easily overburden your body. To successfully handle your toxicity load you have to both reduce your exposure to toxins plus give the nutrients your body needs to neutralise the toxins, so they can be safely carried out via your skin, lungs, urine and faeces.

Increasing the shelf life of food with trans fats, preservatives, extra colouring and so on burdens your liver, inundating it with even more new chemicals without necessarily giving to it the things it needs to cope with them. We all inherit different detoxing capacities, and most people over estimate their reserve. I have heard hundreds of times, 'I used to be able to drink lots and live off pizzas and chips' or something similar. The body needs certain nutrients to cool the fire of certain foods, neutralise their toxicity and get them out of the body safely. If you are constipated you could also be reloading those toxins!

Some of the known beneficial nutrients and foods to support the liver are zinc, molybdenum, iron, copper, magnesium, selenium, vitamin C, extra B5 and B6, cysteine, methionine, taurine, glutamine, aspartic acid, betaine, glutathione, alpha-lipoic acid, omega 3 oils, cabbage, cauliflower, brussels sprouts, broccoli, parsley, kale, watercress, chard, cilantro, beet greens, escarole, dandelion greens and mustard greens, oranges, lemons and limes, garlic, onions, artichoke, asparagus, beets, celery, apples, pears, berries, red and purple coloured vegetables, raw nuts, lean animal protein, eggs, blue green algae, oily fish, olive oil and milk thistle.

The body needs to have sufficient nutrients to function properly. Some food choices are not giving nutrients to the body but actually taking nutrients from the body to process them. Trans fatty acids created by the food industry is an example. The over consumption of alcohol, artificial sweeteners, sugar and salt are others.

If you have habits that include smoking, consuming more than two standard measures of alcohol per day, consuming sweet fizzy drinks (whether using sugar or artificial sweetener) or are taking drugs, you are slowly poisoning yourself and building up your toxicity.

Another way we can take in toxicity is the cleaning and beauty products used for skin and hair care. The body absorbs through the skin as well as releases toxins through our sweat, so we need to be careful. Read labels or check further. Lipstick, for example, not only contains traces of lead but many other contaminating metals. Some women reapply their lipstick twenty-four times a day! When you are not feeling well, the least amount of extra effort your body needs to get rid of toxins the better. So adjust your consumption of these products accordingly.

Your emotional response to situations and thinking can increase the toxic load on the liver. Emotions and thoughts elicit chemical responses in the body. Emotions such as gratitude and compassion can support and nourish the body, neutralising other, more toxic, thoughts and feelings.

5

Skills to Practise
for a Well Life

To move from unconscious coping to engaged participation in the feedback of our own neurocircuitry is a learning process. Learning to notice without judgement and angst, to pause, discern options, experiment and reengage, takes awareness and practice. We can learn to make better choices, manage our limitations and expand our creative options. We don't know our starting point compared to others, so it is a waste of time to compare. What is easy for one is hard for another, and we all have strengths and vulnerabilities. We can each improve and expand ourselves by practising some of the following ideas and methods, which are examples of the many options available to us to enhance our life experience, without drugs.

Mindfulness

Mindfulness is a helpful method of navigation. It helps you to get in touch with your inner compass as well as see the external landscape more clearly. It develops space and integration. It trains our ability to observe and take information from many places within and around us in such a way that we can more easily manage the energy or emotion of that information. It allows us to enjoy the 'now' more, and for change to happen with more ease. As mentioned earlier, inner space helps us to have room in order to sort out the files of information and experiences so they become more easily useful and accessible. We need space to provide buffering from stress, and mindfulness is a tool that helps to build that space within us.

Mindfulness is simple and not so simple. It really is about being fully present in whatever you are doing and observing your thoughts, feelings, sense information and inner sensations from an inner centre, to allow you to be better informed in a balanced way.

Set yourself one 'mindfulness' practice each day. It does not have to take a long time. It is the quality of the experience that matters. That quality of experience moves into the rest of your day over time.

Choose from one of the following and set the amount of time possible without it being a stress.

- MINDFUL EATING: Eat a piece of fruit or vegetable mindfully. Smell it, look at it, admire its colours, give it your full attention and chew it thoroughly. Forget everything else except enjoying and receiving all that is being given to you through the food. You can take it a step further and reflect gratefully about all the effort the rest of the universe has put in so that you could have it.

- MINDFUL BREATHING: Pay attention to your breath, feeling the difference in temperature below your nostril from when you breathe in compared to when you breathe out. See which parts of your body go up or down as you breathe in or out, and notice the connection between what is happening in your body with how you feel and what you think. You can also practice and observe being grateful for the air that is being given to you.

- MINDFUL WALKING: Before you go for a walk, bring your attention to the bottom of your feet and their contact in your shoes or barefoot to the ground. Notice the sensations. Then as you walk, notice the difference when you walk on different surface types, for example, carpet to tiles, pavers to bitumen. Feel the air and sun on your skin as you walk. Look at the beauty around you. Listen to the sound of your footsteps. It is you and the earth making your unique rhythm. Listen to the sounds of birds or animals. Take note of the different aromas. Mindfully walk as often as possible, even if it is for one minute. Walk at a pace you feel comfortable with, and as you change pace notice how your body responds to that. Notice how the air feels on your skin as you change pace. Does the air temperature's effect on you change as you walk faster? How does the sun feel on your skin and eyes? What else do you notice in your environment? What do you notice of other sensations in your body? Do certain thoughts or emotions expand or contract your ability to take in information from your environment? Practice keeping yourself in that observing mindset to allow information to come to you from within and outside, without feeling the need to react to it.

As you practise and learn to differentiate between your thoughts, emotions, bodily sensations—pressure, tightness, temperature and so on—and information from your senses, you will understand yourself more and how you process information. Neutral self-observation allows mental and emotional stability and maturity to develop within. It expands your capacity to self-regulate and respond with a wider range of appropriate emotions and creativity.

The Feldenkrais Method® will teach you about the many ways there are to 'notice' and receive feedback from your body.

Pause

One of the key aspects of wellness living and mindfulness, which has been interwoven through this book, is the 'pause'. It cannot be emphasised enough in the fast-paced life we often live. Pausing to take the time to notice or observe what is happening within yourself and your environment is so valuable. Checking in enables you to participate in giving conscious feedback and adjustment to your nerves and muscles as well as organise yourself for the next step.

Pausing allows us to take an inventory of ourselves, to sort and decide.

We:

- stop

- observe

- connect with our inner resources, others and the rest of the environment

- sort and decide

- and then reengage with some action.

Using your imagination

Your imagination may have opened the way for new possibilities or held you in the grip of fear. I'm here to tell you that harnessing the power of your imagination is a game changer!

So many of the technological achievements we have today came from someone's imagination. Our movies, art, music and stories have all originated from someone's imagination. We can all learn to use our imagination in a more conscious way to impact our health positively.

Your body is responsive to the visual images that you create, whether real or imagined. The other neurons don't know if you have literally seen something or not; they just respond.

They start making the patterns ready for the action that you want. Daily repetition enhances these patterns. Visualisation exercises to mindfully expand your imagination are very worthwhile. One or two periods of 3 to 10 minutes each day add up. It is better to do a little often, than longer periods infrequently.

Choose a quiet place you won't be interrupted and relax by consciously slowing your breath down. Breathe in to the count of four while you watch, or feel with your hands, your belly expand. Hold for the count of three then breathe out for the count of five. Then hold for three again. Do that for three rounds and then bring in a mental image of a relaxed you, competent and enjoying yourself. You can play with it in your imagination and as you practise, bring in more detail or sensory and emotional content to engage more of your neurocircuitry. Finish with one round of conscious breathing as before and return to what you were doing.

Many successful sports coaches encourage their athletes to practise visualisation, using their imagination to give precise detail of, for example, how they are holding their body when they are hitting the ball; where they want the ball to go to; how they feel after the home run; and the sound of the crowd.

A powerful lever for change is created when you connect your visualisation of a desired outcome with a small action that is an aspect of your visualisation. Instead of feeling you have to override your body with willpower to achieve your goal, there is active cooperation from it.

There are two provisos:

- Ensure what you are visualising is in alignment with your core self or unique seed of programming.

- Focus on what you want and not on what you don't want. Always choose the easiest step to visualise and take action on that first, and then develop from there.

Lessons in neuroplasticity

One of the favourite books that I quote to my patients is Norman Doidge (MD)'s *The Brain That Changes Itself.* It is such a hopeful book that illustrates how people's lives have completely changed with new methods that have come from scientists' insights and findings being applied in a clinical setting. They have used high tech MRI scans to see different parts of the brain light up, as well ingenious mirror boxes, to retrain the brain and its influence on different parts of the body. Scientists and doctors used to think the brain did not change and could not be rejuvenated, but this idea has proven too rigid. Yes, it does require effort, but the brain is remarkably adaptive if given the opportunity.

Doidge gives many examples of the power of the imagination to change the brain, how the mind is more than the brain in our head, and how the neuro pathways within the brain and throughout the body are highly adaptive to our environment if given a chance. One example he uses concerns people with 'phantom' limb pain and other sensations even after the amputation of a damaged limb. Previously, many doctors believed that the pain was all 'in their head', or there was 'no hope' which was extremely challenging for the patients. The pain would come when they thought of doing something that would utilise two hands or two legs, depending on which part of the body was missing. One neuroscientist, Ramachandran, developed a method of reducing their pain by asking the amputees to do simple movements repetitively in front of a strategically placed mirror, for fifteen minute intervals. The brain would think it saw the absent limb moving. At this stage it is theorised that the brain is modelling and reorganising its memories around the absent limb from what is seen in the mirror, and is able 'to move on' from the previous last memory of pain. He also found those who regularly visualised in their mind their absent limb moving comfortably had even greater relief from their pain.

This is why I encourage you to rehearse good lifestyle habits to prepare your brain for action. The imagination stimulates new daughter cells in the brain and as you rehearse and practice, you make new neuron connections through your brain, nerves and muscles.

Picture that some of your unhelpful habits are like super highways going in the wrong direction. They may have started for a variety of reasons, but in your brain they have been repeated so much you do them on autopilot. Begin to cultivate an alternative route. Initially, it may be a challenge, more like a goat track through bushland, which is why it can be easy to give up. It takes energy to change. However, change will gradually expand and grow, and the more you can pause and self-correct with kindness when you go down the previous highway, the more the brain will forge new highways. The body is very efficient. It only wants to maintain what is being used, and so it will dissolve disused pathways and just store things as old memories as part of your autobiographical story.

Creating your wellbeing vision

I encourage you to go further in your visualisation and make some visions of possible 'well days'. You may see a typical day in different seasons of the year, or in different stages of your life. In your visions you are safe, at ease, confident, content in yourself and how you are relating to others.

Your vision of yourself is larger than any thought, emotion, situation, diagnosis or opinion of others. Think and reflect about what you really want to experience. See your strengths shining and your vulnerabilities managed. Focus on discovering some 'arrival points'. A GPS requires you to put in your arrival point as well as your current position to be able to suggest different routes for you. We take in so many ideas and influences from others—family, teachers, friends, movies and music—but this is a chance to see what really resonates with you.

The following questions and possible 'ideal day' scenarios are to encourage you to explore options in your mind first. An important aspect of wellbeing is openness to possibilities—recognising and 'owning' that we are an active participant in our own life experience, not just a passive passenger.

What could your typical day look like?

- Who are you living with?

- Where are you living?

- How do you feel when you get out of bed?

- Do you go for a walk, run or do some other exercise?

- What do you have for breakfast?

- What do you put on after your shower or bath?

- Where do you go to work?

- Are you at home or somewhere else?

- How do you get there?

- What do you have mid-morning as a snack?

- What do you have for lunch and afternoon tea?

- When you finish work what do you do?

- What do you have for dinner?

- How do you spend your evening?

- What time do you go to bed?

Here is a possible 'well day' for you to consider and help you imagine your own:

- Being glad to wake up after a restful sleep, open to what the day may bring and looking forward to the day and making your contribution to the collective experience.

- You complete your exercise and walking routine, grateful for the benefit you receive from them.

- You enjoy your healthy breakfast and cleaning yourself, including your teeth.

- You then begin your other activities whether they are paid or unpaid work, study, hobbies, visiting or receiving visitors, appointments and so on.

- You feel the contentment of investing yourself into the activities and the people you are with. It brings both pleasure and meaning, in various ratios.

- You feel safe in your environment and creative in your thinking. As you travel to and fro you notice the nature around you, which gives you strength and energy.

- You enjoy other nourishing meals and regathering times throughout the day. All of the consumables you put into yourself are truly nourishing and without any burden for your body to clear. You also include things that are nourishing for your mind and heart.

- You may do another round of exercise and walk later in the day. You take some time chatting, playing or relaxing with friends or family.

- You feel comfort in your mind, body and spirit and warmth in relationships.

- You are able to reflect and review what you may have learnt that day about yourself, others or your environment. You then plan for and get ready for the next day.

Create your safe place

A very important component of this vision is you are safe. It is vital to create a safe space in your imagination; a place that you can return to and feel safe and comfortable in, no matter what happens in your physical or social environment. It could be a location from some pleasant experience you had or a place from a movie or book. The main thing is you feel good. You feel relaxed, accepted and comfortable. You may want to change this place at another time or maintain the same one. It is up to you. Read the following paragraph then go back in your imagination to your safe place and follow the guideline.

Can you bring the feeling that you see yourself experiencing in your mind's eye, when at this place, into your physical body now? Can you allow the feeling to enter into your lungs and belly and from there spread to all of your body? In your mind trace its path to the top of your head, down your spine to the tips of your toes and back up through your belly to your heart. Feel that you are safe and there are no threats or dangers. You can let go as if you were floating on beautiful, warm water. It may help initially to gently pat or rub your belly, your breastbone and the top of your head to hasten the dispersal of the bracing response to danger from your nerves and body, saying 'It's okay'.

It is a good idea to practise this way of calming yourself each day to build up an associated memory of safety and security within yourself. Really, it's so you have a 'home' inside of you to return to more and more easily whenever you recognise you have moved out of that feeling into tight bracing, from some extended stress response.

If you can practise doing this even for one minute each day, your neuropathways for repair and renewal will be able to work more and more effectively for you.

Advertising to yourself

Let us take this one step further and help you do to yourself what the advertising industry does. Your neurons, throughout the body and brain, store memory by association and so we want to utilize this tendency to bring associations of this safe secure feeling into your present environments. Say your safe place was on a hillside by the waterside, looking over waves and rocks to the beautiful beach. You can hear and smell the waves as well as birds. You can also see other plants growing. So with using these 'mind's eye pictures' as a guide, you could take or buy a photo of such a place, to have at home and your work place. Or you make up a page of cuttings from magazines of your safe place, which you could keep with you. If you have a desk or bench at home or work that you work from, you could put a little rock that reminds you of sea rocks or a little plant or toy animal. The essential point is that when you look at them, you are automatically reminded of your safe place and its impact on your body.

The last, and for many the most potent, is to find an aroma that triggers the memory. You could buy an essential oil of the flower of the plant or a combination spray that immediately takes you to your safe space.

You can use these cues to help you make an environment around you that supports the best in you and others. Watch an advertisement that you liked or stimulated you to make a decision and see what elements impact you, and use them in your prompts.

> *You could even make your own logo and advertise your best self to your stressed self!*

Be a marketing agent to yourself. Work out a symbol, animal, design or aroma that represents what you need to be your true, contented, authentic self. Make a plan around it that you adapt as needed. Then look often at your symbol.

Please pause and take a mental snapshot of how calm feels when you have: a relaxing holiday; time in nature; extended period of leisurely going through your delayed to do list; your favourite home-cooked, lovingly-made meal; a sauna, massage or acupuncture; dancing or exercise session you love; an inspiring gathering ….. Whatever way you can feel completely safe, relaxed and integrated, please pause and take a mental snapshot of how calm feels. Do a full scan of yourself to know this … is … home! *This is where I return to be at my best, and I can return here at any moment in my mind.*

Face worry

Worry is a misuse of imagination. If you are concerned about something, set aside quality time to look at the situation from many angles. Make an initial plan then make an appointment with yourself in three days to review. Then follow on from that by making another appointment for a week after to reflect on whether you need to change the plan. Keep making the appointments with yourself until you have the best plan or the situation is managed. You also can give your plan a name that is relevant to the situation, for example 'Blue Roses', so that whenever stray thoughts come up again from the habit of worry you say to yourself, 'I am following my Blue Roses plan and I am not thinking about the worry now.' If it is a new relevant idea for the situation, write it down for your appointment with yourself. By doing this you retrain your imagination to support you rather than be a hindrance.

The ins and outs of goals

Goals help you achieve your vision. They are a more conscious decision you make. You need to make them understanding that you will be doing them within your bodily intelligence's capability for change. The hypothalamus, which is a key axis part of the brain, nervous systems and endocrine systems interchange, does not like too much change too quickly. It's happy with relaxing stress relief, but if you have held a habit for a long time, you need to expect some resistance. It may come out in you as being more cranky or irritable or as physical symptoms. So as you make your goals, make very small ones initially and build momentum slowly over time. Be willing to revaluate your goals often in the next year.

The keys to effective goals are to make them:

- personal, specific and achievable

- practical and realistic

- possible or reasonable

- measurable—have a timeframe.

Follow the following steps to create a goal that works with your vision. Repeat the steps for each of your goals.

1. Define your goal. Use all your senses to describe what it will look like when completed or accomplished. What will it look like, smell like, feel like, sound like and even taste like!

2. Connect the goal to specific, personally meaningful motives that are primarily intrinsic in nature. Decide what accomplishing the goal this year would mean to you. Your motives will fuel your energy for action.

3. Identify your obstacles to success. You will likely have goals in many areas of your life. Stop—pause! Consider each of them and cross-reference how they

are going to impact each other. Do you realistically have time to achieve them all? Which are the most meaningful? When would you get them done, given your job, family and other commitments?

4. With courage and confidence claim and own your strengths and the resources you have at your disposal to minimise or eliminate your obstacles and resistance.

5. Enlist the support of others; ask for specific help.

6. Expect to take risks and make mistakes. Both courage and humility are essential to success.

7. Artfully balance between structure and flexibility as circumstances change and you become clearer, more focused or better informed.

8. Regularly re-evaluate the goal. Continue what is working and throw out or adjust whatever is not working or is ineffective.

9. Build in ways to celebrate small successes and accomplishments. Most of life is lived while on the journey, not at the destination.

10. Renew your goals as you grow and change through each of the seasons of your life

Helpful habits

We are creatures of habit, so it is a good idea to bring attention and awareness to our habits to see if they are really serving us to be the best we can in our current environment, and if they are leading us towards or away from our goals. Your present habits are based on your previous input from your family, teachers, friends and yourself. Your future habits could be different if you make a decision today to change them.

What you have been doing is based on what you previously knew. The amount of information available today, however, compared to twenty years ago is phenomenal. Choose what is suitable for you now. It may change again and that is okay.

The most critical aspects in successfully building helpful habits are:

1. Preparing a supportive environment around you.

2. Self-correction based around 5 steps:

    a. Pause …
    b. Observe …
    c. Respond appropriately …
    d. Self-adjust …
    e. Take action.

The most important habit to cultivate is to focus on steady improvement. Accepting that we do not jump to mastery of anything allows us to walk the steps we need, one by one.

It will take time to constantly remember to pause, breathe and observe when previously you have found yourself speeding along to where you didn't want to be, feeling overwhelmed by a situation. It will take time to research options that work for you. For example, you may decide to learn yoga and it could take time to find the right style and teacher that suits your schedule.

It will take time ...

... for your nerves to learn how to respond not react.

... to learn to adjust yourself with kindness and not angst and a stick.

... to learn to take the realistic action that can build momentum for you.

Have patience. Not sure what your habits are? Then start tracking...

Tracking to find your pattern

When you see a pattern, you can change some elements of your environment to break associated habits that you want to change. You can free yourself from autopilot to make the choices that serve your wellbeing. You can do this by tracking yourself:

- Take a simple inventory of how you feel when waking; for example, any digestive issues, pains, tightness and discomfort in your body.

- Keep a food, mood and movement diary where you need to ask yourself:

- When do I feel good?

- When don't I?

- What do I do that makes the difference?

- What helps me?

- What hinders me?

- What can I have an impact on?

- What can't I?

- What does a supportive environment look like?

- How can I avoid ones that trips me?

- When do I seek support from others, to get over this hump?

- What am I feeling and learning each day?

- What encourages me?

- What disappoints me?

As an extra note … If after keeping your diary for a week or month you start noticing a pattern of discomfort after eating or using certain cleaning products, there are simple things you can do yourself before you head for expensive tests. One of the easiest is the simple pulse test, developed by American physician Dr Arthur Fernandez Coca. See the appendix for basic information if interested. The other option is to follow an elimination diet for a few weeks, which is best to do with professional guidance. These methods only apply to food sensitivities not anaphylaxis reactions, which are serious medical emergencies.

6

Live with Rhythm

We are part of a rhythm. Life has rhythm: the daily sunrise and sunset; the fluctuations in the moon; the tides of the oceans; the ocean's constant rock with the shore; the seasons of the year. The frequency of the beat may change but it has rhythm.

We also have rhythm. We have activity then rest. We can't be busy all the time and then just collapse. We can't eat all the food we need for a month in two days; it has to be spread out! Some people may have greater capacity to be more active than others, but we all need times to regroup. Even when you ring up tech help, if something goes wrong with your computer or phone network, they tell you to unplug everything and turn everything off so the network can reset itself.

We need pauses, time to rest, regroup, recover, reorganise ourselves and prepare for more activity. There is a time to speak and a time to listen. We have two ears to prompt us to remember to listen to our inner voice as well as the outer environment. This is one reason that *spending time in nature* is so important for your wellbeing, as mentioned in Chapter 3 on nourishment. Seeing and participating in its rhythm helps us find ours again. The frangipani is an example of a plant that goes through a dramatic rhythm through the year. In the cooler months it looks nearly lifeless, but as the warmer weather comes, it puts out its leaves again and then later comes the glorious flowers with their potent perfume. Dogs are always ready for playing or a walk ... but they relax in between!

Filling our lives with *music* is also important. There is a reason it is the universal language. Dancing or moving your body with its rhythm is wonderful for the whole of you. When you walk notice the different beats you and the earth make together on different surfaces. As your pace of walking changes listens to the difference in sounds your feet and clothes make. And let's not forget the nourishment music gives our soul and mind.

Your body is also constantly moving, internally. The sound the heart beat makes is different for each person, much like how your fingerprint is unique. The lymphatic system needs you to move your limbs or breathe deeply for it to circulate. When sitting too long this system becomes congested, making it difficult to move the immune system components quickly and efficiently clear away waste products from cells. The body copes by dumping toxins into fat cells to get them out of the way of its functioning.

Sleep time

Sleep is an extended time of rest where, for example, the muscles that work to keep you upright have a chance to recover. Of course, there is still a lot going on within you during sleep. The night crew come out with their specific duties. Sleep is the time where any repair or growth can take place. It is a very important time for the cells in the gut to repair. It is a challenging environment of food, pollen, pathogens and our immune system, so the lining needs to be replaced every 3–5 days. We have the second highest concentration of neurons in the gut co-ordinating this, so it is important that they have a chance to sort through all the information quietly. This is why a heavy meal late at night is not supporting this need. A lack of appropriate rest enhances the probability of repair not being able to be finished. This can lead to other complications such as not fully digested food components coming through from the gut to the liver and blood. This can then lead to allergic symptoms, chronic inflammation or other issues.

Of course, all the other neurons are sorting out the information that you have been exposed to all day. It is like a busy office with lots of filing cabinets where files of information are going in and out from being used and reorganised. When it is very busy piles of files add up on the tables because there has not been enough 'catch-up' time in between activities to put them back in their folders and cabinets. Sleep is like the catch-up time for you to process and organise sensations, thoughts, feelings and memories. If you make short times of pausing and regrouping throughout the day, this greatly assists the processing and organising. As a consequence your sleep will be more rejuvenating as the sorting and processing burden has not all been left till then.

Worry tends to add lots of little pieces of paper to the table, making it harder to efficiently organise yourself. If you do have a lot of worries, it's a good idea to put aside some quality time earlier in the day to go through, on paper preferably, what the problem really is, what options are available, what is possible, and the pros and cons to make a plan to solve the problem. Make a commitment to a reassessment time in a week. Call your plan a name like 'Blue Roses'. That way if the niggly ideas start up again you have an answer to that noise: ' I have a plan called Blue Roses, which I am following and rechecking on Monday. So if you have an opinion you can tell me then and not before'. This is a good way to clear out the thoughts that come at 3 am in the morning quickly.

It is helpful to make an evening routine so that the associated memories start clicking in that sleep time is coming. As light is a disturbance to the pineal gland, it is important to ensure there is no light, and that there is plenty of fresh air. Also make sure your mobile phone is not right next to your bed. If you must have it in the room place it at least two metres away from you and preferably switched off so you have a break from its electromagnetic radiation. This is an important part of taking care of our own electrical energy. We need to remember each cell maintains itself through various ion pumps and information is transmitted electrically throughout the body, as well as chemically.

It is important to tend to your wellbeing in a loving and kind way to enjoy the fruits of that investment. When you love gardening you just love to be among the plants and dirt. The flowers and vegetables are a wonderful outcome and it is a joy seeing things grow and change with the seasons. There is a part of you that enjoys your growth and change with the seasons of life. If you pause and check in with that part of you even for a very short time often throughout the day, you are going to feel a lot more at peace, happy and protected.

> *If you read a novel without commas, full stops, capital letters and so on, it would be much harder to take it in and find its meaning. It's the same with life. We need pauses to find the meaning*

Progressive relaxation process

Another way to assist getting into a rhythm of activity and renewal is by practising progressive relaxation. Experiment with this technique once or twice a day, varying the time you take from 10 to 15 minutes. It is especially good as part of your night routine. You can take longer, starting at your feet, going up your body and then returning to your toes. Or just go up from toes to head. Sometimes you may want to start the opposite way. It is fine to play with it.

Progressive relaxation enables greater feedback and discernment of tension and relaxation. It enables more effective relaxation to swell up from within the body by purposely increasing the tension, without causing pain, before releasing the tension. It somehow allows that part of the body to know that the work it has been doing has been recognised by 'you', and so it can let go of the information it was holding. Sometimes you may even get an insight later about when or why you became tense, which is useful to help you prepare better for the same situation next time.

I suggest you read the following process and then, if you can, put the book aside and practise before continuing.

- Tighten your feet by curling your toes downward. Hold for 5 to 10 seconds and then release and relax. Stay in the relaxed released stage for 15 to 20 seconds. Use these same time intervals for all other muscle groups.

- Tighten your calf muscles by pulling your toes toward you (flex carefully to avoid cramps). Hold ... and then relax.

- Tighten the muscles in your thighs all the way down to your knees. You will probably have to tighten your hips along with your thighs since the thigh muscles attach at the pelvis. Hold ... and then relax. Feel your thigh muscles smoothing out and relaxing completely.

- Tighten your buttocks by pulling them together. Hold ... and then relax. Imagine the muscles in your hips going loose and limp.

- Tighten your lower back by arching it up. You should omit this exercise if you have lower back pain or issues. Hold ... and then relax.

- Tighten your stomach muscles by sucking your stomach in. Hold ... and then release. Imagine a wave of relaxation spreading through your abdomen.

- Tighten the muscles of your chest by taking in a deep breath. Hold for up to 10 seconds ... and then release slowly. Imagine any excess tension in your chest flowing away with the exhalation.

- Tighten the muscles around your shoulder blades by pushing your shoulder blades back as if you were going to touch them together. Hold the tension in your shoulder blades ... and then relax. Since this area is often especially tense, you might want to repeat the tense-relax sequence twice.

- Tighten your shoulders by raising them up as if you were going to touch your ears. Hold ... and then relax.

- Tighten your triceps, the muscles on the undersides of your upper arms, by extending your arms straight out and locking your elbows. Hold ... and then relax.

- Tighten your biceps by drawing your forearms up toward your shoulders and 'making a muscle' with both arms. Hold... and then relax.

- Clench your fists. Take a few deep breaths and tune in to the weight of your head sinking into whatever surface it is resting on.

- Lift your chin to the ceiling then tuck it down towards your chest and then relax.

- Tighten your jaw by opening your mouth so wide that you stretch the muscles around the hinges of your jaw. Hold ... and then relax. Let your lips part and allow your jaw to hang loose.

- Tense the muscles around your eyes by clenching your eyelids tightly shut. Hold ... and then relax. Imagine sensations of deep relaxation spreading all around them.

- Tense the muscles in your forehead by raising your eyebrows as far as you can. Hold ... and then relax. Imagine your forehead muscles becoming smooth and limp as they relax.

- Lie on your back, with hands and feet apart. Take three deep abdominal breaths, exhaling slowly each time. As you exhale, imagine that tension throughout your body is completely flowing away.

7

Other Essential Components

Good choices

When you make helpful choices from what you take in from your environment, you ensure easier nourishment and elimination of waste. This includes your food, water, music, media you watch or read and the people you hang out with. There are some people or things that are hard to avoid yet you know they take away more energy. So make wise choices when you can. Also the more you focus on the constructive choices you can make for yourself, the more encouraged and empowered you feel. With the people and things you can't avoid, prepare yourself for them as best you can and pause afterwards to fully recover your inner balance.

Inner team and outer team

It also helps to see yourself as a team and that you are also part of a bigger team. Let us look at a football club as an example. What builds the spirit of that club? The short answer is more than one thing. Yes, some people may emphasise a certain player, or players, or the coach or management, its history, the fans. But it really is the combination of all these things and more. On any given day one part may stand out more, but for the club to really have a great spirit all the parts need to work together respectfully, and each part has its place in the whole club.

You are the captain of your team of cells and systems on every level of you, and at the same time you are a member of a bigger team. You are the point of connection for the circles of care.

We each need a combination of family, friends, educators and health professionals with whom we can share openly and receive guidance. You can't say everything to everybody, but you need to be able to open your heart and mind fully to be in relationship with others. Be on the lookout for your support team, and how you are a member of someone else's support team.

Awareness

Recognising the value of developing your awareness of yourself, your environments and your interactions with them will open opportunities for expansion that nothing else or no one else can give you. Awareness will enable you to discern and differentiate accurately what happens within yourself—the sensations, feelings and thoughts you are having and what is happening in your environment and how they influence each other. After a while clear patterns will emerge.

Ask yourself, 'What happens in me, whatever the environment, and what happens only in certain environments or with certain people?' This can help you to recognise which places and people you need to spend more preparation for and recovery time. This informs your choices more easily and helps you to stay more confidently aligned with who you truly are. To be frank, some people take more energy to process, just as it takes your lungs a longer time to recover from breathing in polluted air than fresh air.

We can learn to see our adaptions to the environment. Some adaptions are okay for a short period or occasionally, and others can be all right for the long term. Some may have worked for our ancestors or kept us alive, or our reserves of energy could tolerate them when we were young, but not as we get older.

From looking at your pattern you can learn what associations you have stored in your memory bank. Are they accurate or from limited perception? My children have said as they got older that they remember thinking how enormous our backyard was when they were little, and now it does not look so big at all! There are many things that we need to re-evaluate in the light of more experience and be willing to let go of in order to make more room for 'now'. Without letting go, our capacity does not increase but, on the contrary, decreases. Awareness helps us to recognise our own unfinished business of processing. If the same feeling keeps on coming up under different circumstances and with different people then the common denominator are your filters of information. Your perspective, values, beliefs and experiences can open or close pathways of rich information and experience.

Get involved in something that matters to you

One of the ironies of wellbeing is that even though you are spending a lot of time noticing what and why you are doing actions, to be really well you also need to get involved and forget yourself through total investment or engagement with something bigger than yourself that you love. It could be part of a community garden, sporting club, hobby group, religious or spiritual group, paid or volunteer work, playing music or singing in a choir, as examples.

Move your body

Do things you really enjoy, like dancing, walking, yoga, Feldenkrais or swimming. Don't focus on what you can't do or don't like, but what you can and are fun. Do any activity that will safely help to improve your wellbeing.

Learn about the Pandiculation movements, which help to release tension by resetting your neurons in your brain and nerves for relaxation or new action. You can start by looking at how dogs and cats move before and after sitting or lying down!

The structural, electrical and chemical aspects of how we function and regulate ourselves benefit from movement such as our lymphatic system, which is a network of tubes throughout the body that drains fluid (called lymph) from tissues and empties it back into the bloodstream. It is one of the managers of fluid levels in the body and white blood cells of the immune system as well as the recipient of our absorbed fatty acids from the small intestine. Lymph is filtered through the spleen, thymus and lymph nodes before being emptied into the blood. It does not have a pump like the blood vessels; it is moved by us moving. Deep, rhythmic breathing, moving our arms and legs and body brushing all help it. Without movement it is easy to develop swelling, especially in the legs, as fluid accumulates. It then tends to become congested with cellular waste products too large to return directly to the bloodstream for excretion, which is not helpful when fighting bacteria and viruses. As well we release endorphins after movement. There is the biochemical aspect of this as well as the satisfaction we feel when our mind and body co-operate.

You need to start slowly if you have not been doing any exercise for a while. It might be good to get a personal trainer to ensure you proceed step by step and not do so much the first couple of days that you can't do anything for a couple of months! Managing injury is a very important aspect.

I personally walk each day, practice Dr Joseph Weisberg's 3-Minute Maintenance Method for optimal musculoskeletal function and a selection from meridian harmony movements or qigong practices. I always feel better within myself after than before. Many times I seemed to have walked a problem or worry away. I also do a Feldenkrais class weekly. I have found it helps me do all the others more effectively.

Movement is also of benefit to supporting our bioelectricity. Every cell has a sodium/potassium pump to help transport in and out its nourishment and waste products, and the neurons transmit between each other electrically as well as chemically every message. Our moving through the earth's magnetic field helps ours to be better balanced.

Our bodies function and organise themselves through electrical and chemical activity. Electromagnetic energy is constantly being produced in the body through biochemical reactions in food and air assimilation, and circulated by electromotive forces within the body. In addition, you are constantly being affected by external electromagnetic forces such as that of the Earth or the electrical field created by the clouds.

Your heart has its own internal electrical system that controls the rate and rhythm of your heartbeat. With each heartbeat, an electrical signal spreads from the top of your heart to the bottom. As the signal travels, it causes the heart to contract and pump blood. The brain, heart and gut neurons together make a large electromagnetic field around us. We are aware of this field as we meet each other even on an unconscious level.

Moving your body is a natural stress release helping the autonomic nervous system to reset to balance. With that your hormones release endorphins to help you feel better. Moving also helps you to engage with the natural rhythm of life, which is constantly moving. The latest research is showing that sitting too long has a worse outcome on your metabolism than smoking! Even getting up for a minute every couple of hours when working to move your body will make a huge difference to how you feel at the end of the day. Remember, something is a quantum leap from nothing!

Practise reconciliation principles

Saying 'sorry' and 'please forgive me' opens the way for love and gratitude to be received and given. The Ho'oponopono Hawaiian healing process is powerful. We held a weekly meditation and discussion program for a year centring on the Ho'oponopono process of repeating the four phrases, 'I'm sorry', 'I love you', 'Please forgive me', 'Thank you'. Participants practised saying the phrases to themselves as well as others during the week. In our gathering we would sing the phrases and then have a time of quiet meditation, going over the phrases silently in our mind. We then shared, so we could learn from each other what we had experienced that evening and during the week.

Examples of what was shared

- 'Instead of going into an internal dialogue when I felt upset, I started the phrases which calmed me down.'

- 'I felt like my soul was emerging through layers of dust that were being dispersed.'

- 'I could feel the waves at the beach saying, "I love you" to me, encouraging me.'

- 'I have found that it is loosening old emotional pain in me, so it is not as debilitating and I can more easily feel grateful.'

- 'It has taken my attention away from blaming or accusing someone to finding solutions to problems.'

- 'I am becoming kinder to myself.'

- 'I find I am becoming more open in situations.'

One aspect that was often discussed, especially by people new to the process, was the difference between saying 'I forgive you' and 'Please forgive me'. Our conclusion was that asking 'Please forgive me' was a more open invitation to someone to go further together with them.

8

How to Apply Your Learnings

When you do feel well, light and just good in yourself, take a mental snap shot. This is home. You are at home in your body, in your environment. Check in with how your breathing is; how your neck, shoulders and belly area feel. By doing this it is easier to return to and reload the memories and the associated physical sensations into yourself. You could also take it a step further and, as mentioned previously, choose some little stone, toy or other item that you can associate with feeling your calm energised self. Put this on your desk or up on a wall to look at and gain confidence whenever you need to regroup. Likewise choosing an associated aroma that you can spray or put on your wrist as part of your preparation or recovery routine is powerful.

Learn to listen to your body's prompts. Sharpen your discerning abilities between its physical needs, its response to danger from outside sense information or from your thoughts and feelings from memories, worries or reactions to people. This then helps you more consciously provide appropriate feedback into your body's communication circuits.

Learn to notice the connections between your bodily sensations, the information from your senses, and your thoughts and feelings. This helps you to work more supportively with your innate self-regulation capacity.

Track yourself with journals or diaries especially around your food choices, moods, who you are with and the environment. This helps you to find patterns more clearly that you can then adjust to help yourself better.

Listen to your self-talk and what you say to others, to learn more of what is inside of you. Once again what you notice you can work with. Always 'notice' softly, with kindness to self and others. This reduces reactivity. The more reactivity you have the more extra layers you have to process before you can resolve what you noticed!

Make a vision that all of you can unite with. That is, it includes the parts of you that are focused on survival, protecting you from danger, the parts that wants social connections for pleasure and meaning, and the creative you. All of your systems need to find a way to co-operate respectively so they can all make their contribution in sustaining and enriching your life. Each part serves you in some way.

Use your imagination constructively and play with it to visualise 'you being well', including your ideal daily routine (not a holiday but normal life for you), over a week, a month and a year. Build up to a longer time of visualisation by putting aside regular time each day to visualise; to clear up different scenarios in your mind. Layer more detail and emotion into it. It will change and that's good as it comes to reflect the fruit of your greater capacity to be in touch with who you uniquely are and what you have to contribute to the bigger picture. It is better to focus and train your imagination this way than let it mull in worry. The more you go into the detail the better. From the detail you could find little elements to bring into today. For example, if you see yourself moving to certain music, start playing that today.

From your vision make firm and achievable goals and plans. These may range from the next day to weekly, monthly and longer term. Include re-evaluation steps for reflections and processing in those plans.

Show up fully into your life and activities, even the seemingly mundane. Practise being fully present, investing in the variety of activities and experiences that are in your day.

Be prepared to do regular internal housekeeping, asking with a kind openness, 'Do I really need this in my life anymore? Does this idea, feeling or attachment really serve me to be my best anymore?' If the answer is 'no', keep showing it the door till it gets the message. It is more important to fulfil the purpose of an activity than the method used. Connect to the purpose or meaning of a relationship or activity to see what is appropriate for this time period. As with regular housekeeping, it is easier to do a little regularly than leave it for long periods.

Make your own rhythm, routine and rituals to make sure you keep yourself on the track of balance.

Nurture your circles of care. You have both inner and out circles that need your attention.

Practise belly breathing and rubbing to counter bracing of this area.

Learn to notice, self-adjust and apply when you have had a slip up. Avoid getting lost in internal angst or resorting to denial.

Mindfully walk as often as possible, even if it is for one minute.

Find people to whom you will regularly share openly about how you are. They could be a professional health practitioner, coach, mentor, parent, friend or colleague.

Remember, you have two ears for listening, and within the inner ear is your sense of balance. Figuratively, one ear is for your inner self and the other for the outer environment.

Here is a checklist of reminders and affirmations to include in your daily routine to maintain focus on the quality of daily experience:

- I am practising kindness.

- I regularly look at my symbol that represents my well integrated self.

- I practise mindfulness throughout the day as well as extended set periods in the day.

- I nourish myself well on the mind, body and spirit levels.

- I practise planning, preparing, recovering and reflecting around my daily life.

- I look after and am involved in my circles of care.

- I manage my frustrations and disappointments proactively and safely.

- I take pauses, rests and sleep regularly.

- When there is a strain in a relationship I practise the reconciliation principles.

- I walk and move as much as I can every day.

- I look for the good and inspiring around me each day, recognising that I and all are being given to by the rest of the universe every day.

- I receive with gratitude and give with joy.

Ask yourself:

- How did I nourish myself today?

- What did I learn?

- Who did I learn it from?

- How's my processing going?

Things to put more attention on to bring more wellness into your life today:

- the ever changing beauty of the sky

- uplifting music

- mindful walking

- mindful eating

- belly breathing

- slower breathing

- making someone else happy, even by simply making them the type of tea or beverage they like

- growing a plant or two

- having a pet

- listening and caring for someone

- reflecting on whether what you are doing today will bring you closer or further apart from wellness tomorrow

- finding the meaning in the simple things you do every day and how that is contributing to the bigger picture

- taking the time to pause and notice what you in your being, with others and the environment, are experiencing. Do you need to regroup to your core, knowing centre?

- making an environment around you that supports your best

- avoiding sugary drinks and limit consumption of high-calorie foods, especially those low in fibre and rich in fat or added sugar and chemicals

- eating a broader variety of fresh food not processed. Have vegetables as the main component with protein at each meal. Always have breakfast.

- learning your pattern of tightness, where in your body, and how to release it by learning the way you relax

- finding the laughter, fun and joy in your day.

Self-evaluation

In which directions are you headed?

As previously mentioned your wellbeing capacity is dynamic. The central question for us is "If I keep acting, speaking or thinking as I am now, is my capacity increasing or decreasing?" No judgement, just kind objectivity – looking at where you are – "I am here". Some days or parts of days may be increasing and others decreasing.

The following nine indicators will give you a quick, clear gauge and are also something that you can adjust yourself through. For example, if you notice that you are complaining in your mind or words about a situation, others or yourself, to neutralise that and change direction focus on something you are genuinely grateful for and expand from there.

Low capacity	High capacity
Unmanaged disease process	Managed disease process
Isolation	Connection
Stagnation	Movement
Dismissive	Respectful
Reactive	Responsiveness
Complaint	Gratitude
Criticism	Compassion
Extreme external or internal focus	Balanced internal or external focus
Filler	Nourishment

9

Final Word

The understanding and appreciation of the inner knowing we all have has been growing over the years. Many of our greatest current technological breakthroughs first came from someone's hunch or quiet observations. Confidently use your inner knowing—your own connection to the body's wisdom. If something works for you to have more peace and satisfaction use it. Don't wait for science, technology, medicine or your current culture to catch up and confirm that you were right. Trust your inner knowing and act on it. Bring it out into your daily life and others will benefit too, as well as you!

About the Author

Tracy De Geer is a passionate advocate for proactive wellbeing care. Her passion and knowledge have developed over a 40-year love of learning about health and wellbeing. Her journey began initially as a patient, and then while looking after her family of five children and being involved in volunteer community work. For the last 20 years she formalised her study and has worked in various clinical settings. Tracy has a Health Science Degree (Complementary Medicine) from Charles Sturt University, NSW, Australia as well as an Advanced Diploma in Naturopathy from the College of Somatic Studies Qld, Australia.

Tracy began working at Nature Care Wholistic and Medical Centre 15 years ago part-time, and five years ago she became the Director. She has seen a wide variety of patients in different stages of their wellbeing, from seriously ill to those seeking the optimum development of their potential. Tracy continues to develop her knowledge and skill base through attending seminar and reading journals, which include medical and natural healing and wellbeing journals.

Tracy can be contacted at: *www.naturecarewholistic.com.au* and *www.vibrant-contentment.com*.

Appendix

The Coca test is self-administered and follows a simple procedure. First, take the pulse fourteen (14) times per day for three (3) days as follows: once before getting out of bed, once before each meal, 3 times after each meal at 30 minute intervals and just before bedtime. The duration of the pulse recording must be one full minute. All pulses should be taken while sitting except for the first, which is taken immediately upon waking. Record all results and the contents of each meal. Snacks should be avoided, but, if eaten, their contents and the pulse should also be recorded.

In evaluating the results, please note that the daily low pulse rate is normally equivalent to the waking rate pulse rate (the exception being when a suspected allergen is in the bed). So first, make note of the highest and lowest pulse on each day. Normally, the maximum range difference is 16 beats. A higher rate indicates that an allergen has been encountered.

Next, calculate the average pulse, as well as the differential (the difference between the daily low and high rates).

Anything that causes variation from the differential is a suspected allergen.

If an increased pulse after a meal is noted, a dietary sensitivity can be present. To determine which substance is the cause, eliminate select elements of that meal and test again. Foods raising the resting pulse over 12 beats per minute above the morning resting pulse indicate a suspected allergen and should be eliminated.

Resources

1. Essential SOMATICS – Pain Relief Through Movement www. essentialsomatics.com

2. Pandiculation www.gravitywerks.com

3. The National Institute for the Clinical Application of Behavioural Medicine – Brain Science www.nicabm.com

4. Moshe Feldenkrais: 'The aim is a body that is organised to move with minimum effort and maximum efficiency, not through muscular strength but increased consciousness of how it works.' Look up your local classes.

5. *3 Minutes to a Pain-free Life* by Heidi Shink and Joseph Weisberg.

Printed in the United States
By Bookmasters